# Inside Out

## My Book About

### Who I Am and How I Feel

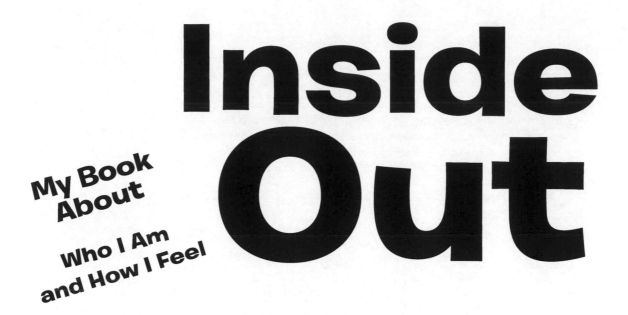

This journal belongs to

_____

by

# Gretchen Van Kleef

**BALBOA**
PRESS
A DIVISION OF HAY HOUSE

Balboa Press books may be ordered through booksellers or by contacting:

Balboa Press
A Division of Hay House
1663 Liberty Drive
Bloomington, IN 47403
www.balboapress.com
1 (877) 407-4847

Because of the dynamic nature of the Internet, any web addresses or links contained in this book may have changed since publication and may no longer be valid. The views expressed in this work are solely those of the author and do not necessarily reflect the views of the publisher, and the publisher hereby disclaims any responsibility for them.

The author of this book does not dispense medical advice or prescribe the use of any technique as a form of treatment for physical, emotional, or medical problems without the advice of a physician, either directly or indirectly. The intent of the author is only to offer information of a general nature to help you in your quest for emotional and spiritual well-being. In the event you use any of the information in this book for yourself, which is your constitutional right, the author and the publisher assume no responsibility for your actions.

Any people depicted in stock imagery provided by Thinkstock are models, and such images are being used for illustrative purposes only.
Certain stock imagery © Thinkstock.

Print information available on the last page.

ISBN: 978-1-5043-9606-6 (sc)
ISBN: 978-1-5043-9607-3 (e)

Balboa Press rev. date: 02/06/2018

# About the Author

Gretchen Van Kleef has a master's degree in clinical psychology and many years of counseling experience. She has worked with individuals and families with a wide range of problems, including stress-related problems and substance abuse. She is passionate about helping young people feel good about themselves and develop coping skills.

# Contents

# Dedication

This book is dedicated to the memory of my mother, Alfhild Van Kleef, who loved me dearly and taught me to believe in myself.

# A Note to the Reader

Dear Friend,

I hope this journal helps you know yourself better. There are no right or wrong answers to any of the questions.

Please do page one of this journal first. Page one helps you think about where you've been and where you're going.

After page one, you can go to any page you want. If you have a special problem or feeling or topic you are thinking about, look on the Contents pages. You may find something that fits your mood. Some of the pages in this journal can be done together if you wish. For example, Pages 46 and 47 are both about "affirmations." You may want to do those on the same day or week.

Try setting aside a quiet time once a day or once a week. Find a private, peaceful place and give yourself lots of time to read, think, and write. If you get angry or upset after filling out certain pages, find someone to talk to about your feelings. There are ideas for people you can talk to at the end of this journal (page 94). These are caring people who are willing to listen.

Enjoy yourself!

# How We Feel About Ourselves

Date:

How happy we are is often determined by how we feel about ourselves. Sometimes it helps to make a list of all the feelings we have about ourselves. Then we can find ways to like ourselves more.

▲  How I felt about myself half a year ago:

▲  How I feel about myself today:

▲  How I'd like to feel about myself:

*I wish I felt better about myself. But I do like myself more than last year.*

# Finding Our Good Points

Sometimes we forget how good we really are. It helps to write down good things about ourselves. They remind us what great people we are.

▲  My good qualities:

*I am really kind to people. Sometimes I help
the lady who lives across the street.*

# Other People Can Affect Our Self-Esteem

Date:

Other people can make a big difference in how we feel about ourselves. If someone says, "You're smart. You can do that," we feel good. If someone says, "You're stupid" or "You're ugly," we feel bad. Sometimes we feel better if we stop being around people who make us feel bad.

▲  People who make me feel good about myself:

▲  People who make me feel bad about myself:

▲  Do I still need to be around the people who make me feel bad? Do I have to believe what they say?

*I stopped paying attention to what Jordan says,
because it always made me mad or sad.*

## Comparing Ourselves to Others

Sometimes we try to make ourselves feel better by comparing ourselves to other people. We may feel we are "better than" some people, but we usually end up feeling "worse than" other people. When we compare, we aren't appreciating the special people *we* are.

▲  Times I compared myself to other people:

▲  How did that make me feel?

*It felt good when I told myself I was smarter than my brothers, but then I remembered how many kids are smarter than me.*

4

# Setting Personal Goals

Many people feel good when they are working toward a goal that is important to them. A goal could be learning to play the piano, becoming a better basketball player, or making new friends. Goals are best when they are *our* goals, not things other people want us to do.

▲  Goals I accomplished last year:

▲  My goals for this year:

*This year I'd like to get better at soccer. My parents*
*want me to play baseball, but I'd rather play soccer.*

# How Other People Can Help

Sometimes things get in our way when we work on goals. That makes it hard to keep working toward our goals. It helps to know other people who have goals like ours so we can help each other.

▲ People who might have goals like mine:

▲ Ways we might be able to help each other:

▲ Other people I can look to for help:

*My friend Brittany is really good at math. I can ask
her to help me so I'll make better grades.*

# Worrying About New Things

Sometimes we worry about things that are new or different, like moving to a new neighborhood, going to a different school, or trying a new haircut. Most of the time when we do something new or different, things turn out fine. Sometimes we are even happier than before.

▲ Times I did something new and different:

▲ Which of these changes turned out okay?

▲ Which of these changes didn't turn out okay?

*I moved to a different part of town and I was worried about going to a new school.*

# Imagining the Worst

Some of us always think the worst will happen. If a friend gets mad at us, we think that friend won't like us anymore. If we make one bad grade on a test, we think we will fail the whole class. If we take a trip by plane, we fear the plane will crash. By imagining the worst, we keep ourselves worried and upset.

▲ One thing I am worrying about:

▲ What is the worst possible thing that could happen?

▲ What are some other things that could happen?

*I worry about Carlos getting mad at me and
never coming to my house again.*

# Getting Unworried

When we are worried, it helps to talk about our worries – or write them down. Then we can put them aside for a while. After we write a list of our worries, we can tear it up. Or we can put it away in a drawer or a special "worry box," where we put everything we want to let go of. Then we can get busy doing something else and forget about our worries.

▲  Worries I want to get rid of – things I really can't *do* anything about:

▲  How I will let go of those worries:

*I want to stop worrying about my mom*
*when she goes out of town for work.*

# Worries that Went Away

Sometimes, when we look back, we realize that many of our worries just went away. Things we worried about in the past no longer worry us now. Sometimes we found something to do about what we were worrying about. Other times we let go of our worries, and the situation took care of itself.

▲ Things I used to worry about that I no longer worry about:

▲ Worries I did something about:

▲ Worries that went away by themselves:

*I used to worry every year before school started.*
*I worried I wouldn't like my teachers. But it's*
*always been okay, so I don't worry anymore.*

# Getting Honest

Everyone does nice things and not-so-nice things to other people. Sometimes it's hard to be honest with ourselves about the times we've hurt someone else.

▲ Nice things I have done for other people:

▲ How I felt about myself when I did things that were nice:

▲ Things I did to other people that were not nice:

▲ How I felt about myself when I did things that were not nice:

*I was really nice to the new girl at school. I invited her to sit with me at lunch. I wasn't very nice to my sister last week.*

Most of us tend to get angry and upset when things don't go exactly the way we want them to. Sometimes the things that don't go our way turn out okay.

▲ Things I got upset about or didn't like at first that later turned out to be okay:

*I got really mad when my dad wouldn't let me spend the night with Chris. But it wasn't that bad staying home.*

# Being a Secret Helper

Doing nice things for other people is one way to feel good about ourselves. We might even do something nice and not tell anyone about it. That way we won't be doing it to get something in return, or so people will tell us how nice we are. It can be our little secret, one that makes us feel good about ourselves. That's really fun!

▲ Something nice I could do for someone without anyone knowing:

*I could take out the trash and not tell anyone.*

# Being Good to Ourselves

Being good to ourselves is just as important as being good to other people. It's a way of showing love to ourselves.

▲ Good things I have done for myself:

▲ Other good things I want to do for myself:

*When I start putting myself down, I stop and*
*think something good about myself.*

# Trusting Other People

Sometimes things happen that make us afraid of other people. We may believe we can't trust anyone. But as we get older, we learn we can trust certain people. These are the people that care about us and respect our feelings.

▲  People I can trust:

▲  How I know I can trust them:

*I can trust my grandparents, because they are always nice to me and tell me they love me.*

## Trusting the Wrong Person

We all make the mistake at times of trusting someone who disappoints us. Maybe the person agreed to do something and he or she didn't do it. Maybe we told the person a very special secret and he or she told other people. This is how we learn who to trust and who not to trust. It's a normal part of learning about friends and other people.

▲  People I have learned not to trust:

▲  What they did to show me I couldn't trust them:

*We speak Spanish at home and I heard Allison making fun of my accent to her other friends. I can't trust her anymore.*

16

# Talking About Problems

Most of us have some things we don't want to talk about. Maybe our parents fight or someone is picking on us or we don't like the way we look. It helps to write those things down and find one special person to share them with.

▲ Things that are easy to talk about:

▲ Things that are hard to talk about:

▲ Someone I can talk to about the hard things:

*My dad yells at everyone when he's drinking.*
*I can't talk to anyone about that.*

# A Wonderful World

Most of the time we don't look at things around us. But some days, we *really* see how wonderful the world is. We look at the sky in the daytime or the stars at night, and we suddenly *feel* how big the world is. It fills us with wonder.

▲   Times I have felt wonder at the world around me:

▲   How I felt about being alive in those moments:

*I saw a beautiful sunset yesterday. It reminded me what a wonderful world I live in.*

# Parents Aren't Perfect

Date:

Our parents are human, like everyone else. They do some things we like and respect - and probably some things we don't like. As we grow up, we can follow their good example in some ways, and learn to be different from them in other ways.

▲ Things I like about my parents - ways I would like to be like them:

▲ Ways I would like to be different from my parents:

*My parents are really smart and have good jobs.*
*I want to have a good job when I grow up.*

# Good Friends Make Us Feel Good

One way to feel good about ourselves is to be around people who love and appreciate us. These people know our faults and still like us. They are good friends.

▲ People I feel good with because I know they really like me:

▲ What they say and do that I like:

*My friends Jennifer and Jada really like me. They tell me they like me and they want to spend time with me.*

# Picking Friends

In picking a friend we want someone we can talk to, someone who is honest, someone we can depend on, someone we can trust. We may want the person to share our interests and activities. There may be other special things we look for in friends. We make our lives happier by picking our friends carefully.

▲ The kinds of things I look for in friends, especially good friends:

*It is easy to be friends with someone*
*who likes the same things I do.*

# Making Friends

Making friends comes naturally to some of us. Others find it hard to let people get to know them. We can work to change that, if we want to. We can start getting to know a new person by doing things together. We can talk about things we both like, and later share some special things about ourselves.

▲ Would I like to change anything about how I make friends?

▲ Is there anyone I'd like to become better friends with?

▲ How can I start to become friends with that person?

*I'd like to be friends with Jamie. Maybe I could talk to him and see what things he likes to do.*

# Being a Good Friend

Being a good friend to other people is important. It includes many things: talking with our friends about their interests and feelings, being ready when they need help or need to talk, and telling the truth about how we feel. If we think about what we want in a friend, that's usually what other people want too.

▲  Ways I am a good friend:

*I am a good friend because I can tell when my friends are sad and I try to cheer them up.*

# Learning to Laugh at Ourselves

Date:

Laughter can lift our moods and make our troubles fade away. Sometimes it is hard to laugh at ourselves. If we make a mistake or do something silly (which we all do at times), we worry that we have "made a fool of ourselves." We are happier when we laugh about those things and go on.

▲ Times I took myself too seriously:

▲ Times I was able to laugh at myself:

*I took myself too seriously when I messed up my lines in the play. But later I could laugh about it.*

## Sensing Our Power

Most of us have done things that were hard to do – and succeeded at them. It gives us a wonderful sense of our own power. We think, *If I can do that, I can do anything!* It gives us new confidence to try other things that might be hard for us.

▲  Hard things I did that I succeeded at:

▲  New things I want to do:

*Playing the trumpet seemed really hard
at first, but now I'm good at it.*

# Accepting Ourselves

All of us would like to change something about ourselves. If we have good self-esteem, we like ourselves anyway, despite our faults. Some things we can work to change are the way we act, who our friends are, or how we feel about ourselves. Other things, such as what we look like, can't always be changed. These things we learn to accept and love about ourselves.

▲  Things I would like to change about myself:

▲  Things I can't change about myself that I will try to accept:

*I think my nose is too big, but I'll try to accept it.*

# Changing Ourselves

Date:

It takes patience and work to change things about ourselves. This is true whether we want to be a better friend, find a new hobby, become a better athlete, make better grades, or get along better with our brothers and sisters. We can change if we do just a little bit each day.

▲ One thing about myself I want to change:

▲ What I will do today to start working on this:

## Look at this page in one month.

▲ How I changed in the past month:

*I'd like to stop getting angry so much. I can think about something else when I start to get mad.*

# My Dream Picture

Lots of times we can't change unless the *picture* we have of ourselves changes. We can help ourselves change by imagining *in detail* who we would like to be. What do we want to be good at? How do we want to spend our time? Who do we want as friends? How do we want to dress? How do we want to feel about ourselves? All change starts with the vision of where we are going.

▲   My dream picture – the kind of person I'd like to be, the kind of life I'd like to have:

*I'd like to be popular and have lots of friends. I can imagine
I'm at school and everyone wants to talk to me!*

# Being Grateful

Every day contains things – some big, some small – to be happy about: the good things people do for us, things we accomplish, a sunset we see, a book we enjoy, a hug from a friend. These things make us feel good.

▲  Good things in my day today:

*We got out of school early and I got to go to Dalton's house. That was cool.*

# Taking Risks that Help Us

A risk is something we haven't tried before. Often we must take risks in order to learn new things. A risk can be big or small. It might mean talking to a new person, dancing, playing a new sport, or learning to sing. It can be fun to challenge ourselves and take risks.

▲  Risks I have been afraid to take:

▲  Risks I have taken that helped me learn new things:

*I took a risk by taking a hard class I didn't
have to take. I learned a lot.*

# Taking Risks that Hurt Us

Date:

Sometimes we take risks and do things that might hurt us or other people. We think it is okay because "everybody does it." We don't stop to think about what might happen as a result.

▲ Risks I have taken that hurt (or could have hurt) me:

▲ Risks I have taken that hurt (or could have hurt) other people:

*I smoked part of a cigarette once. That hurt me. It made me sick.*

# How We Take Care of Ourselves

Part of good self-esteem is taking care of our bodies. When we feel good physically, we feel energetic and full of life.

How I take care of myself physically:

▲ Overall

▲ Eating habits

▲ Exercise

▲ Sleep

▲ Other

*I'm not very good at taking care of myself. I eat
a lot of junk food and stay up too late.*

# Caring About Our Appearance

Part of good self-esteem is caring about the way we look. We feel better about ourselves if we are clean and dressed neatly. Most of us have special things that help us feel good, such as fixing our hair a certain way or wearing clothes we love. These things can give us a little boost on days we are feeling down.

▲   How do I show I care about my appearance?

▲   Are there special things I do that always make me feel good?

*When I curl my hair before school, I always feel good.*

# What to Do When We're Feeling Bad

We all have ways of making ourselves feel better when we're feeling upset or mad or sad. These might be taking a walk, talking to a friend, writing in a journal, soaking in the bathtub, drawing pictures of our feelings, or working on our favorite hobby. It is important that we find the ways that work best for us.

▲ Things I can do to feel better when I'm feeling bad:

*It always makes me feel better when I draw funny pictures, like cartoons.*

# Taking an Interest in Things Around Us  Date:

Sometimes we spend so much time thinking about our lives and our feelings that we hardly see what is happening around us. Taking an interest in other things can help us feel better. When we take our minds off ourselves, some problems don't seem so bad.

▲  How I take an interest in other people:

▲  How I take an interest in things in my school, home, or community:

▲  How I take an interest in things in the country and around the world:

*Sometimes I watch the news with my parents.*

# Trusting Our Intuition

The main way we know things is through our senses of sight, hearing, smell, taste, and touch. Many people also believe in a "sixth sense." We call this our *intuition,* our "gut feeling." Intuition can tell us things about ourselves and other people. For example, we might sense that the new kid in school will become our best friend. We might have a "funny feeling" around a certain group of people and know we need to stay away from them. We might have a hunch that we will love playing tennis, even though we've never tried it.

▲ Examples of intuition in my life:

▲ How my intuition helped me:

*One of my uncles gives me the creeps, so I stay away from him.*

# Facing Our Fears

Everyone has fears. Some fear is good because it protects us, such as the fear of getting in a car with a driver who's been drinking. Other fears that many of us have are speaking in front of class, meeting new people, or trying a new activity. These are the kinds of fears we can work to overcome. One of the best ways to get over a fear is just to do whatever we are afraid of. After we do it a few times, the fear usually goes away.

▲  One fear I have:

▲  Things I could do to start overcoming that fear:

▲  What I will do today to start overcoming that fear:

*I'm afraid the teacher will call on me in class. I guess I could study more. Then maybe I wouldn't be so scared.*

## Things We Used to Be Afraid Of

When facing our fears, it sometimes helps to think of the things we were afraid of in the past. Many of those fears have disappeared. If those fears went away, the fears we have today can also go away.

▲ Things I used to be afraid of that I'm not afraid of today:

▲ How I overcame those fears:

*I used to be afraid of the water. I kept getting in the pool anyway, and now I'm not scared.*

# Accepting Things We Can't Change

There are many things in life we can't control or change. We can't control what other people do, or change many of the things that happen to us. Sometimes we just have to accept those things. The only things we can change are our attitudes and our behavior.

▲ People and things I can't control or change (that I wish I could):

▲ How I can change my thinking to feel better about these things:

*I don't like people always saying how tall I am. I could tell myself I will like being tall when I'm grown.*

# Keeping Promises

Part of feeling good about ourselves is keeping our promises to people. This means doing what we say we will do and being where we say we will be. Most people feel better about themselves when they keep their promises.

▲ How do I feel about myself when I do what I say I'll do?

▲ How do I feel about myself when I don't keep a promise?

▲ Is there anything I need to do today to keep a promise I made?

*I promised my mom I'd clean my room*
*after school today. I need to do it.*

# Promises That Should Not Be Kept

Once in a while a friend tells us something really bad and swears us to secrecy. Maybe that friend is being abused, or is thinking of hurting themselves or someone else. Even if we promised not to tell, sometimes we really do need to tell someone.

▲  Has anyone ever told me a secret like that?

▲  What was the secret?

▲  Did I want to tell an adult about it? Did I?

▲  What could I do about it now?

*My best friend told me her dad beats her. I didn't tell anyone,*
*but maybe I will now. She still looks sad all the time.*

# Honesty Makes Us Feel Good

Date:

Nobody is honest all the time. Sometimes we say things that aren't true, like "little white lies." Sometimes we are dishonest by covering up our true feelings. Most of us feel a lot better when we can be honest.

▲  A time when I was dishonest with someone, and how I felt about it:

▲  A time I was honest, even though it was hard to do:

*When I sneak around and lie to my parents, I feel bad.*

# Making People Read Our Minds

Sometimes we think our best friends or people in our families should *know* how we feel, so we don't tell them. This can lead to misunderstandings and hurt feelings, when they don't know how we feel or what we want. It's not fair to expect people to read our minds.

▲   A time I wanted someone to guess how I was feeling or what I wanted:

▲   What happened in the end:

*My best friend hurt my feelings so I stayed away from him. I thought he'd figure out why I was upset, but he never did.*

## Putting Ourselves Down

Many of us, without knowing it, say hundreds of things to put ourselves down: "I'm dumb"; "I'm not as pretty or handsome as so-and-so"; "I can't do that"; "No one likes me." Some of these things we say to other people. Others we just think to ourselves. That kind of talking and thinking hurts us! Knowing that we talk about ourselves this way is the first step toward changing it.

▲ Things I say or think to put myself down:

*I tell myself I'm dumb when I make a bad grade.*

44

# Feeling Jealous of Other People

Sometimes we feel jealous of other people. Maybe they have nicer clothes or fancier houses than we do. Maybe they have more friends. Maybe their moms and dads still live together (and ours don't). Feeling jealous is just one way we put ourselves down and make ourselves feel bad.

▲ Have I been jealous of someone else? For what?

▲ How did that make me feel?

▲ If I still feel jealous, what can I do about it?

*I can tell myself it doesn't matter if Jessica lives in a nicer house. Someday I can live in a really nice house, too.*

# Affirmations

One way to change the negative things we think about ourselves is to write out and say *affirmations*. An affirmation is something good we say to ourselves over and over again. If we think of ourselves as dumb, our affirmation might be *I learn quickly* or *I'm smart*. In an affirmation, we say something is already true about us (*I am smart*, not *I will be smart*). Every time we catch ourselves thinking, *I'm dumb,* we stop and think, *I'm smart.*

▲  One thing I say to put myself down:

▲  A positive affirmation I can say instead:

**Now say that affirmation ten times out loud. Say it with feeling, because you really believe it.**

▲  Other positive affirmations I can say about myself:

*I tell myself I'm too thin and I don't have any muscles.*
*I could tell myself I'm getting stronger every day.*

# Making Our Affirmations Come True

One way to help our affirmations come true is to think about how we will look, feel, and act when we are what we want to be. For example, if our affirmation is *I am smart,* we imagine how confident we will feel when we are studying, answering questions in class, or taking tests. Once we start believing our new, positive thoughts, we will automatically make small changes to make those positive thoughts come true.

▲ Spend five minutes or more thinking about the new you in your affirmation. Write down what you imagined.

*I imagined lifting weights and getting stronger and stronger. Then people started saying I looked strong.*

# Saying No

Sometimes people get trapped into doing things they know aren't right because they have a hard time saying no. This might be doing someone else's homework, lying to cover up for a friend, or drinking alcohol or using other drugs.

▲   Times I got trapped into doing things I knew weren't right:

▲   What would have happened if I said no?

▲   Are there certain people I have an especially hard time saying no to? Why?

*I have a hard time saying no to Katy, because*
*I want her to still be my friend.*

# Practicing Saying No

Saying no is easier if we think about it and practice it ahead of time. What do we want to say no to? Will we just say no, or will we say something more? Often we can suggest something else to do, something we both feel good about.

▲ Something I want to say no to in the future:

▲ What I will say when I am asked to do this thing I don't feel good about:

▲ Other things I could suggest to do:

*I want to say no to smoking and taking drugs. I could say I have to leave.*

## Thoughts and Feelings

How we think about things determines how we feel about them. For example, what do we tell ourselves if we don't get to go somewhere? If we think, *This is awful! I'm the only person who doesn't get to go!* we will make ourselves miserable. If we think, *That's too bad, but there are lot of things I can enjoy doing at home*, we won't feel so bad.

▲  Something I felt bad about recently:

▲  What I thought about it, what I was telling myself about it:

▲  What else I could have thought about it, so I would have felt better:

*I felt bad because my parents didn't have the money*
*for me to go on a trip with my friend. I could think about*
*how to earn my own money so I could go next time.*

# Thinking We're "Terrible" at Something Date:

Sometimes we think we're "terrible" at something because we don't do well at first. We think that because something was true once, it will always be true. If we don't do well the first time we try to play baseball, we think, *I'm a terrible baseball player.* If we do one thing we wish we hadn't done, we think, *I'm a terrible person.* When we think like this, we often stop trying to be better. We can often be successful if we keep trying, making all kinds of mistakes, until we get better.

▲  Something I think I'm "terrible" at:

▲  How could I go back now and try to get better at it?

*I'm terrible at playing the piano. But I could start practicing again and see if I'm better.*

Most of us do things that don't work. Maybe we argue with our parents about the same things over and over. Maybe we continue to be afraid to ask for help when we have problems at school. Maybe we try over and over to be friends with someone who isn't friendly to us. Instead of doing those things, we could decide to do something totally different – like not arguing, or asking for help, or finding other friends. It might work better.

▲ Something I have done over and over that didn't work:

▲ Is there something I can do in that situation that is completely different from what I have done in the past?

*I get mad every time Mikayla doesn't want to come over. I could invite someone else instead.*

# Compliments

How do we feel when someone says we're smart, or dressed nicely, or good at doing something? Some of us feel funny when people say nice things about us. We don't think we deserve the compliments. But we can start believing the good things people say about us. We can smile and say "Thank you." Compliments can help us feel good about ourselves.

▲ Nice things people have said about me:

▲ The compliments I found it hard to believe or accept:

*I don't know what to say when people say I'm pretty.*

# How We Feel About Ourselves:
# A Checkup

Date:

Sometimes it is good to look back and check our progress. We often find we have made more progress than we were aware of day to day.

▲ How I feel about myself overall:

▲ Things I did or learned this past month that made me feel good about myself:

▲ What I still want to work on:

▲ What I will do today to work on those areas:

**Now check your answers to the questions on page one to see your progress.**

# Breaking Big Goals into Little Goals

Sometimes we feel overwhelmed by the big things in life – the big goals we have set for ourselves, the big changes we want to make. When we feel that way, it is easy to give up and do nothing. We need to remember that the big things will get done if we just do a little bit toward them each day.

▲   A big goal I have for myself (in any area of my life):

▲   One small thing I can do today to work toward that goal:

*I want to become an engineer and build bridges and big buildings. I could work harder to make good grades in math.*

# Rewarding Ourselves

Having a reward to look forward to often helps us get things done. We can reward ourselves in many ways. We can watch a movie after our schoolwork is done. We can visit a friend after we finish our chores. We can buy something special for ourselves when we make a good grade. One of the best rewards is "patting ourselves on the back" – being proud of ourselves, and then telling someone else about the hard work we have done.

▲ Ways I can reward myself when I have worked hard:

*I can talk on the phone when my schoolwork is done.*

# Easy Does It

Date:

Many of us get worn out when we try too hard at certain things. We can tell the difference in working "hard" and working "too hard" by how we feel. If we are working hard on something, we feel good, even great. If we are working too hard, we often feel worn out, exhausted. It's good to tell ourselves, *easy does it*. It reminds us to relax and enjoy ourselves, even when we are working hard on something.

▲ Times I was probably working too hard:

▲ How I felt when I was working too hard:

*I was studying so hard to make A's that
my stomach hurt all the time.*

# Our Feelings Affect Our Bodies

Different emotions make our bodies feel different. When we are happy, we often feel light, like we have all kinds of energy. When we are angry or afraid, our stomachs may get upset. We may find our throats tightening up or our hands getting clammy. We may get a headache. Everyone is a little different in how their bodies react to their feelings.

How my body feels when I am:

▲  Happy

▲  Angry

▲  Sad

▲  Afraid or worried

*When I'm afraid, I can feel my heart pounding.*

# Harmful Ways of Dealing with Anger

All of us at times get frustrated or angry about things that happen. There are both helpful and harmful ways of handling those situations. A harmful way, for example, is getting mad and kicking a chair. The person who does that will probably end up with a hurt foot – and maybe a broken chair.

▲ Ways of handling anger that are harmful or don't accomplish anything:

*It doesn't accomplish anything to yell and scream when you're mad, especially if you're yelling at a teacher.*

# Helpful Ways of Dealing with Anger

There are helpful ways we can deal with our anger. We don't cover it up, but we do find ways to express it that won't hurt us or other people. Instead of screaming at the person we are mad at, we sit down and explain our side of things. Or, we run or play soccer to work our anger off, instead of kicking a chair.

▲ Helpful ways of dealing with anger:

*It's better to explain your side of things and why you're mad.*

# How Important Is This?

One question we can ask when we're upset it, "How important is this?" Some things really *are* important enough for us to get angry or upset about. Other things that upset us *seem* important at the time, but aren't very important once they are over. Asking ourselves "How important is this?" helps us remember that everything isn't important enough to get upset about.

▲ Several things that upset me recently:

▲ Which things weren't important in the end?

▲ Which things are still important today?

*It upset me when Jill didn't sit with me at lunch. In the end it didn't really matter.*

Sadness is part of everyone's life. We are sad when someone close to us dies, or when a friend moves away. We are sad when we aren't getting along well with a friend. We are sad if our parents get divorced.

▲   Things that have made me sad:

*I was very sad when my grandfather died. I miss him a lot.*

# Expressing Our Sadness

Some people find it easy to express sadness, while others find it hard. Some people may tell us, "Be strong; you can handle it; you don't need to cry." So, we try to hold our sadness in or pretend we aren't sad. By doing that, we stay a *little* sad all the time. But if we let the sadness out, it often goes away and we feel better.

▲  Ways I can let my sadness out:

*I can cry and talk to one of my friends about it.*

# Dealing With Extreme Anger or Sadness

Date:

Some of us get so angry or sad that we want to lash out in violence, either against ourselves or other people. That kind of violence can ruin our lives, as well as hurting other people. If we feel that way, the best thing to do is tell someone and get help for those feelings.

▲ Have I ever been so upset that I wanted to be violent toward myself or other people?

▲ What did I do about it?

▲ What can I do now, if I still feel that way?

▲ Have I ever heard anyone threaten that kind of violence? What did I do about it?

*I overheard someone say he wanted to kill himself. I got scared because his dad has guns. I told one of my teachers. I think he got some help because he seems happier now.*

# We Are Unique

Each of us has something special inside of us – the part that is really *us*. We are the only ones who have the exact personality and talents that we do. It makes us different from our family and friends, different from any person who has ever lived. It is great to really *feel* what a special person we are.

▲  The ways I am unique and special:

*I am unique because I'm really good at playing chess. I'm also unique because my mom is black and my dad is white.*

# Being Ourselves

Date:

All of us play-act from time to time, putting on a role, rather than just being ourselves. If we do it a lot, it probably means we're scared to be ourselves because we're afraid other people won't like us. We will be happier when we learn to be ourselves around other people. Of course, it's easier to be ourselves when we're with people we know and trust.

▲ Times I am myself:

▲ Times I play a role, not letting people know the real me:

▲ People I can be myself with:

*I sometimes play a role at school,*
*pretending I feel okay when I don't.*

# Roles We Play in Our Families

Date:

One place we often play roles is at home. Without knowing it, we learn to act in certain ways. Some of us are always "nice" or always "responsible." Some of us are the "troublemakers" or the "loners." Some of us are the "peacemakers," trying to stop arguments. Some of us are the "clowns," trying to make people laugh. Some of us are the "counselors," listening to problems. Some of us can play *all* these roles.

▲  What roles do I play with members of my family?

▲  Do I play these same roles outside the family (with friends or at school)?

▲  Do I like playing these roles? Would I sometimes like to act different? How?

*In my family, I listen to everyone's problems. I don't like it when my mom and dad tell me their problems.*

# Believing in Ourselves

In some of our families, we are encouraged to become all we can be in life. Others of us have families that don't encourage us as much. But all of us can believe in ourselves and search out special friends who also believe in us. This is especially important if we're not getting the support we need from our families.

▲ Do members of my family support and encourage me in becoming all I can be?

▲ Do *I* believe in myself? Do *I* believe I can make my dreams come true?

▲ Do I have special friends who believe in me?

*My best friend always tells me I can make*
*better grades if I just study more.*

# Self-Confidence

Most of us feel more confident about some things than others.

▲ Things I almost always feel confident about:

▲ Things I sometimes feel confident about:

▲ Things I almost never feel confident about:

*I always feel confident about my schoolwork. I almost never feel confident about sports.*

# Building Our Self-Confidence

Date:

We can build our self-confidence by trying new things, even if we don't succeed at first. We can tell ourselves we have confidence in ourselves, even if we don't at first. With practice, we will get better, and our confidence will grow.

▲ Something I would like to have more confidence about:

▲ Things I can do to start building my self-confidence in that area:

▲ Which one of these things can I do today?

*I would like to have more confidence about my
singing. I could start by singing in the shower
or when I'm alone in my bedroom.*

# People We Can Depend On

Date:

All of us need other people to depend on. This is true whether we are young or old. Many of us have families who will always be there for us when we need them. Others of us have to look for people outside our families to depend on. It's helpful to keep a list handy and to call these people whenever we need a friend. They could be school friends, cousins, relatives, teachers, or other special people.

▲ People in my family I can depend on to care about me or take care of me:

Other people I can depend on:

| Name | Phone Number |
|------|--------------|
| | |
| | |
| | |
| | |

*I can depend on my family and my neighbor next door. She has liked me a lot since I was a little kid.*

# Depending on Ourselves

Some of us have learned at an early age to take good care of ourselves by making meals, doing laundry, or other things. This independence can be good and can help us feel more confident. Sometimes, though, it can feel like too much to handle.

▲ Ways I have learned to depend on myself:

▲ What I like and don't like about my independence:

*I have to make my own breakfast every day
because my parents leave early to go to work.*

# How We Handle Freedom

Most of us are given more freedom to do things as we get older. But sometimes our parents don't feel we act responsibly, and they take some of that freedom away.

▲ Freedom I have now that I didn't have a few years ago:

▲ Has any of my freedom been taken away (even for a short time) because my parents didn't agree with how I handled it?

▲ Would I do anything differently in the future to convince them I can handle the responsibility?

*I can stay over at my best friend's house more than I used to. One time I didn't call when we went somewhere, so I couldn't go back for a month. Next time I'll call!*

# Blaming Other People

Some of us have the habit of blaming other people for what's happening to us. We blame teachers for our bad grades, instead of admitting we didn't study much. We blame a friend for not doing something, instead of admitting we never asked him or her to do it. Blaming others makes us feel weak, as if "the world is against me" or "nothing goes right for me." Taking responsibility makes us feel stronger. We know we can handle the situation better next time.

▲  A time I blamed someone else for something that happened to me:

▲  How could I feel stronger by taking responsibility for that situation?

*I always blame my brother for starting our fights. But I start some of them. I could act better and not get in so many fights.*

# Blaming Ourselves

Date:

Some of us have a habit of blaming ourselves for too many things. We blame ourselves for things that aren't our fault. We blame ourselves if bad things happen to us, or if someone is mean to us. We blame ourselves if our parents get divorced. We will be happier if we learn not to blame ourselves for these things. Instead, we need to separate what we *are* responsible for from what we are *not* responsible for.

▲  Things I blame myself for:

▲  Which of these are things I couldn't control?

▲  Which ones could I control?

*I blamed myself when my parents were having problems.*
*But then I learned I didn't cause their problems.*

# Dealing with Other People's Bad Moods Date:

From time to time we all have to deal with people who are in a bad mood. These could be our parents, teachers, friends, or neighbors. Some of us get mad at the person for being in a bad mood; some of us get scared by it; some of us let the person's bad mood put us in a bad mood; some of us start wondering what we did wrong to cause the person's bad mood.

▲ How I usually react when someone else is in a bad mood:

▲ Do I react differently around some people in a bad mood than around others in a bad mood?

▲ Is there another way I could react to people's bad moods?

*I get scared when my dad is in a bad mood because he's*
*so loud and grouchy. I could take some deep breaths*
*and remind myself he doesn't stay this way forever.*

76

# Our Family's Unwritten Rules

Different families have different unwritten rules. For example, in some families, children are expected to make top grades. In other families, they are expected to do well in sports. In some families, children are expected *not* to succeed. In others, they are expected to be just like their parents.

▲   The unwritten rules in my family – what is expected of me:

*My parents expect me to make A's and go to college.*

# Our Family's Rules About Talking

Most families have unwritten rules about how the people in the family talk to each other. In some families, children are to be "seen and not heard." In other families, they are encouraged to talk about feelings and problems. In some families, children learn they are supposed to keep certain things secret. In some families, people are taught not to disagree or have arguments.

▲ The kinds of things we talk about in my family:

▲ The kinds of things it is not okay to talk about:

▲ Are the "rules" about talking different for me than for other members of the family?

*It's not okay to talk about how much my parents fight.*
*My mom told me not to tell my grandma about that.*

# How Our Families Express Feelings

Different families have different ways of expressing feelings. In some families, people yell and scream when they are mad. In other families, people go off alone and don't talk when they are angry. In some families, people pretend they never get mad. In others, only certain people are allowed to express their anger.

How other people in my family express:

▲ Anger

▲ Sadness

▲ Happiness

▲ Fear

*When my dad gets sad, he leaves the room and doesn't talk to anyone for a long time.*

# Expressing Our Feelings

Part of feeling good about ourselves is learning to feel and express *all* our feelings - anger, sadness, joy, and fear. We can choose to express them the same way as other members of our family, or we can express them differently.

▲ A list of *all* the feelings I have - happiness, silliness, anger, jealousy, and other feelings:

▲ Which ones are hardest for me to feel?

▲ How do I express these feelings?

*It's hard to feel silly because I'm usually pretty serious. And I don't like to let myself feel sad. I'm afraid I'll feel really, really, really sad.*

# It's Great to Be Alive

Being alive is often wonderful. We all have special moments when we feel the joy of just being alive. It might be when we first wake up on a sunny morning, or when we skip down the street, or when we sit quietly watching a fire or a sunset or a baby playing. It's a feeling that comes from deep inside us and makes us feel great.

▲   Times I feel especially good just being alive:

*I felt great when I was at camp and making new
friends and doing lots of things outdoors.*

# Expressing Our Love

Some of us find it hard to say "I love you." It's a good habit to tell our families and friends how special they are to us. It feels good to tell people we care about them – just as it feels good to hear that other people care about us.

▲ People who are really special to me, people I love:

▲ Have I told them lately how special they are to me?

▲ What can I do *today* to show one of these people how I feel?

*I love my parents, my grandma and my sister. I never tell my sister I love her.*

# Being Happy

Abraham Lincoln said, "Most folks are about as happy as they make up their minds to be." He didn't say, "Folks will be happy if everything is perfect in their lives." He didn't mean we should ignore our angry or sad feelings. He meant that people can always find things to be happy about, if they try.

▲ Things I can be happy about today:

*I made a passing grade in science. I was happy about that.*

## Growing Up Is Confusing

Growing up is often confusing. One day we feel grown-up, the next day we feel like little kids. Our bodies, minds, and feelings are always changing. Sometimes we're not sure how we're supposed to feel or act. It often helps to talk to other people (people our own age or grown-ups) about our feelings.

▲  Things I find confusing or hard to deal with at my age:

▲  People I can talk to about these feelings:

*I was <u>really</u> confused when my parents got divorced. And I'm confused about boys and whether I want a boyfriend.*

# Arguing with Brothers and Sisters

Almost all of us get into arguments at times with our brothers and sisters. When that happens, do we run to our parents wanting to be told we're right, that we're the "winner"? Sometimes there's a way to work things out between ourselves so that everyone wins. (If you don't have brothers or sisters, think about how you settle arguments with your friends.)

▲ A time I argued with a brother or sister (or good friend):

▲ Was there a "winner" and a "loser" in this situation?

▲ How could we have settled the problem so that everyone "won"?

*I argue with my sister a lot. Sometimes we both end up upset and no one wins.*

# Learning to Handle Money

One of the skills we need as we grow up is the ability to handle money. This means we spend carefully and save for the things we want in the future. It may mean we are careful in other ways, such as not lending money to people who haven't paid us back in the past. It also means we learn how to give ourselves a special treat now and then – just because we deserve it.

How I handle my money:

▲  Saving

▲  Spending

*When someone gives me money, I spend too much on little stuff. Then I don't have money for the big things I want to buy.*

# Familiar Things to Hang On To

Most of us like having familiar things and people in our lives, especially if we are going through a big change or having problems. If we are moving to a new town, we feel good knowing that other members of our family will be there with us. If we are having problems at home, we feel good knowing that our favorite teacher or best friend will be at school for us to talk to.

▲  A time when I went through a big change or had a lot of problems:

▲  What people in my life stayed the same during that time?

▲  What activities in my life stayed the same?

*It was a big change when we moved to Texas.*
*But my family stayed the same and I got to*
*do gymnastics again in my new town.*

## Being Careful About Other People's Advice

Date:

We can often get good ideas about things from talking to our friends. But we need to decide for ourselves whether we want to follow their advice or not. Sometimes other people's advice is good for us. Other times it is not. One way to tell if advice is helpful is to imagine what would happen if we followed the advice.

▲   A time when someone gave me good advice:

▲   A time when someone gave me advice that wasn't so good:

*Someone told me to sneak out of the house at night. That wasn't a good idea!*

# Showing Appreciation to Our Parents

Most of us have a parent or parents who have a lot of responsibility. They have to work to earn money. They have to make sure we have food to eat and a place to live. They spend a lot of time taking care of us. It is nice to show our parents we love and appreciate them for all the things they do.

▲ Things my parents do to care for me:

▲ Things I could say or do for them to let them know I appreciate them:

*I tell my parents every night that I love them.*

## Making Chores Fun

Most of us have chores to do around the house, such as keeping our rooms clean, or taking out the trash, or cleaning the bathroom. Sometimes we don't feel like doing them. Since we have to do them anyway, we can look for ways to make them more enjoyable. We might even be able to have fun doing them. Some people get together and help each other with chores. Others play music they like, or make a game out of the chore.

▲  Ways I could make my chores more enjoyable:

*I really like to play music. Maybe that would help when I have to vacuum.*

# Taking Quiet Time for Ourselves

Date:

We all need quiet time - time to be by ourselves and slow down from the day's activities. It gives us time to think about things, plan things, or daydream about things we want to do. It helps us feel rested and refreshed.

▲  Do I take quiet time for myself every day?

▲  What do I enjoy doing or thinking about in my quiet time?

*Sometimes I like being by myself. I can read science fiction or daydream about things.*

# Seeing the Good in Other People

Date:

Sometimes it is easier to see the things we don't like in people than the things we do like. The things we don't like about them seem to stand out more than the things we like. But everyone has good points, just like we do. We can sometimes feel better about a person we don't like if we remember his or her good points.

▲ Someone I think of in a bad way:

▲ How I feel when I am around this person:

▲ The person's good points:

▲ Would I feel different around this person if I tried to remember his or her good points?

*There's a kid in my class I can't stand. I think he acts stupid.*
*But he's really nice to the boy who's blind, so that's good.*

# Our Heroes

Many people have heroes they look up to. For some people, their heroes are people they know and admire, such as their parents or teachers. For others, their heroes are people who are famous, either people who are alive today or people in history. Heroes help us see what kind of people we can become.

▲ My heroes:

▲ What I admire about each of them:

*I like Superman. He's just an ordinary guy with problems, but then he saves the world.*

# Here are some people you might call when you need to talk to someone:

▲ Mom or Dad

▲ Brother or sister

▲ Friends

▲ Cousins or other relatives

▲ Priest, reverend, minister, rabbi

▲ Teacher

▲ School counselor

▲ Friendly neighbor

▲ Librarian

▲ Police or call 911 (for emergencies or if someone is hurting you)

▲ Al-Anon or Alateen (if someone you love drinks too much alcohol or uses drugs)

▲ Alcoholics Anonymous (if you use alcohol or drugs)

▲ Family service agency in your city or county

▲ Social service agency in your city or county

Some names of important people and their phone numbers:

| **Name** | **Phone Number** |
| --- | --- |
|  |  |
|  |  |
|  |  |
|  |  |
|  |  |
|  |  |
|  |  |

Printed in the United States
By Bookmasters